My First
Italian
Lesson

Color & Learn!

Illustrated by
Roz Fulcher

ballare
bah-**lahr**-reh

Dover Publications, Inc.
Mineola, New York

This handy book will have you speaking Italian in no time! More than sixty illustrated pages include commonly used words and phrases in both Italian and English. Below each Italian word or phrase you'll find its pronunciation. A syllable that is **boldfaced** should be stressed.

Whether it's just for fun, for travel, or to have a conversation with a friend or relative, you'll find out how to talk about the weather, tell what you'd like at mealtime, and many other helpful phrases—and you can color while you learn!

Bibliographical Note

This Dover edition, first published in 2019, is a republication in a different format of the work originally published by Dover in 2015 as *Color & Learn Easy Italian Phrases for Kids*.

International Standard Book Number

ISBN-13: 978-0-486-83311-8
ISBN-10: 0-486-83311-9

Manufactured in the United States by LSC Communications
83311901   2019
www.doverpublications.com

Hello. Good-bye.

See you later.

What's your name?

Ecco
eh-koh

1. mia madre
mee-ah **mah**-dreh

2. mio padre
mee-oh **pah**-dreh

3. mia sorella
mee-ah soh-**reh**-lah

4. mio fratello
mee-oh frah-**teh**-loh

This is my   1. Mother   2. Father
              3. Sister   4. Brother

How old are you?

I am _____ years old.

I'm allergic to nuts/eggs.

What's for breakfast?   1. Cereal

2. il toast
eel toast

3. le uova
leh **woh**-vah

2. Toast

3. Eggs

È l'ora di pranzo. Voglio . . .
eh **loh**-rah dee **prahn**-zoh. **voh**-lee-oh

1. un panino
oon pah-**nee**-noh

It's time for lunch. I want. . .

1. a sandwich

2. un yogurt
oon **yoh**-gert

3. un hamburger
oon **ham**-bur-gur

2. Yogurt   3. Hamburger

I'm hungry! What's for dinner?

1. Pollo?
poh-loh

2. Pesce?
peh-sheh

3. Pizza?
pee-tzah

1. Chicken?   2. Fish?   3. Pizza?

What's for dessert?

1. Gelato?
jeh-**lah**-toh

2. Frutta?
froo-tah

3. Biscotti?
bees-**koh**-tee

1. Ice cream   2. Fruit
3. Cookies

4. andare in bicicletta
ahn-**dah**-reh een bee-chee-**cleh**-tah

3. disegnare
dee-seh-**nyah**-reh

3. Draw   4. Bike

Can you help me, please? I'm lost.

Buon Natale!

bwon nah-**tah**-leh!

Merry Christmas!

Felice anno nuovo!

feh-**lee**-cheh **ah**-no **nwo**-voh!

Happy New Year!

This is delicious! I'd like some more.

Where are you from?
I am from _____.

25

I giorni della settimana

eeh **jor**-nee deh-lah set-tee-**mah**-nah

Monday  *lunedì*
loo-neh-**dee**

Tuesday *martedì*
mahr-teh-**dee**

Wednesday *mercoledì*
mehr-koh-leh-**dee**

Days of the week

Thursday  *giovedì*
joh-veh-**dee**

Friday *venerdì*
veh-nehr-**dee**

Saturday *sabato*
sah-bah-toh

Sunday  *domenica*
doh-**meh**-nee-kah

I mesi
eeh **meh**-see

January
gennaio
jeh-**nah**-yoh

February
febbraio
feb-**brah**-yoh

March
marzo
mahrt-zoh

April
aprile
ah-**pree**-leh

May
Maggio
mah-djoh

June
giugno
joon-yoh

Months

luglio
lool-yoh

Agosto
ah-**goss**-toh

settembre
set-**tem**-breh

ottobre
ot-toh-breh

novembre
noh-**vem**-breh

dicembre
dee-**chem**-breh

I numeri
eeh noo-**mare**-ee

uno
oo-noh

due
doo-eh

tre
treh

quattro
kwaht-troh

cinque
cheen-kweh

Numbers

sei
say

sette
set-teh

otto
ot-toh

nove
noh-veh

dieci
dee-**eh**-chee

I colori
eeh coh-**lor**-ee

Green
verde
vehr-day

Red
rosso
roh-soh

Blue
blu
bloo

Colors

Yellow
giallo
jah-low

Colors

White
bianco
bee-**an**-koh

Black
nero
neh-roh

Orange
arancione
ah-ran-**choh**-nay

Purple
viola
vee-**oh**-lah

Gray
grigio
gree-joh

1. How much does it cost?
2. It's one dollar.

Let's go to the beach! I will get . . .

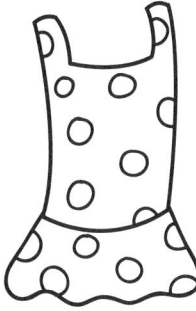

1. il costume da bagno
eel coh-**stoo**-meh dah **ba**-nyo

2. la crema solare
lah **creh**-mah soh-**la**-reh

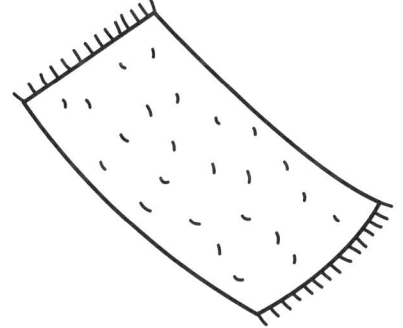

3. il telo
eel **teh**-loh

1. my bathing suit   2. my lotion
3. my towel

Thank you.   You're welcome.

Could you speak more slowly?

It's hot today. I'll wear . . .

1. una maglietta
oo-nah mah-lee-**eh**-tah

2. i pantaloncini
eeh pahn-tah-lohn-**chee**-nee

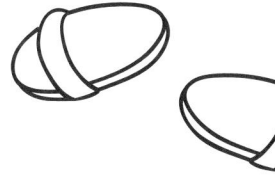

3. i sandal
eeh **sahn**-dah-lee

1. a T-shirt   2. shorts
3. sandals

1. una sciarpa
oo-nah shee-**ahr**-pah

2. i guanti
eeh **gwahn**-tee

3. gli stivali
luh-yee stee-**vah**-lee

4. un cappotto
oon kah-**poh**-toh

1. my scarf
3. my boots

2. my gloves
4. my coat

I'm cold. I need . . .

1. una maglia
oo-nah **mahl**-yah

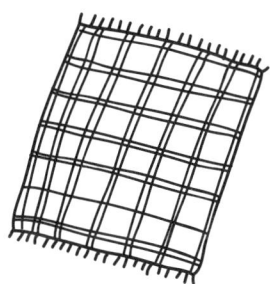

2. una coperta
oo-nah coh-**per**-tah

3. una giacca
oo-nah **jah**-kah

1. a sweater   2. a blanket
3. a jacket

I'm thirsty. I want . . .

1. l'acqua
lah-kwah

2. il succo
eel **sooh**-koh

3. il latte
eel **lah**-teh

1. water   2. juice   3. milk

Excuse me.

1. *Dov'è il ristorante
più vicino?*
doh-veh eel
ree-stoh-**rahn**-teh
pyoo vee-**chee**-noh

2. *Dov'è la fermata
dell'autobus più vicina?*
doh-veh lah fair-**mah**-tah
dehl-auto-**boos**
pyoo vee-**chee**-nah

3. *Dov'è la metropolitana
più vicina?*
doh-veh lah
meh-tro-po-lee-**tah**-nah
pyoo vee-**chee**-nah

Where is the nearest ... 1. restaurant?
2. bus stop?   3. subway?

Do you have a pet?   I have . . .

1. un cane
oon **kah**-neh

2. un gatto
oon **gah**-toh

3. un pesce
oon **peh**-sheh

4. un uccello
oon oo-**cheh**-
loh

5. un criceto
oon kree-**cheh**-toh

1. a dog   2. a cat   3. a fish
4. a bird   5. a hamster

Happy birthday! My birthday is in

_____.

1. guardare la TV?
gwahr-**dah**-reh lah tee-vooh

2. andare al cinema?
ahn-**dah**-reh ahl
chee-neh-mah

3. andare fuori?
ahn-**dah**-reh **fwo**-ree

Posso . . .
poh-soh

Can I . . . 1. Watch TV?
2. Go to a movie? 3. Go outside?

1. nonna
noh-nah

2. nonno
noh-noh

3. zia
tsee-ah

4. zio
tsee-oh

5. cugina
ku-**jee**-nah

6. cugino
ku-**jee**-noh

1. Grandma
2. Grandpa
3. Aunt
4. Uncle
5. Cousin (girl)
6. Cousin (boy)

I don't feel well. My . . . 1. throat
2. head   3. stomach . . . (hurts)

I'm tired. Time for bed.

Good night.